R U ?

a dedicated pRanK sTaR?

Check the **boxes** then **add up** your score.

A day without pranks is . . .

- [ ] like a day without chips. **(2)**
- [ ] like any other day. **(1)**
- [ ] not worth getting out of bed for. **(3)**

Which of these could you not live without?

- [ ] Joke book **(2)**
- [ ] Fake bug **(3)**
- [ ] Math homework **(1)**

Your sister is about to go on a date and you notice a rather attractive booger hanging from her nose. Do you?

- [ ] Tell her right away. **(1)**
- [ ] Keep it zipped and watch the booger boogie! **(3)**
- [ ] Offer a tissue and let her do the math. **(2)**

add up your scores and turn to page 57 for the results (if you can be bothered...)

Doodle some hairs sprouting from the wart.

uNLeaSHeD!

Hands off!
It's mine!

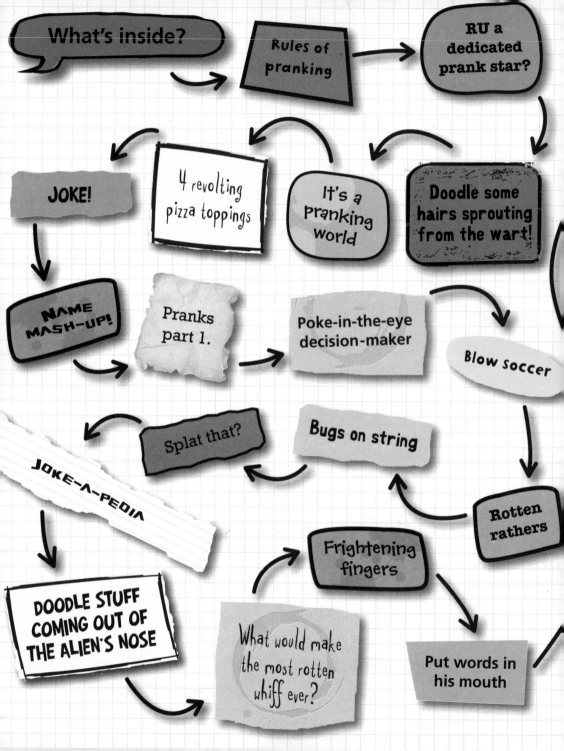

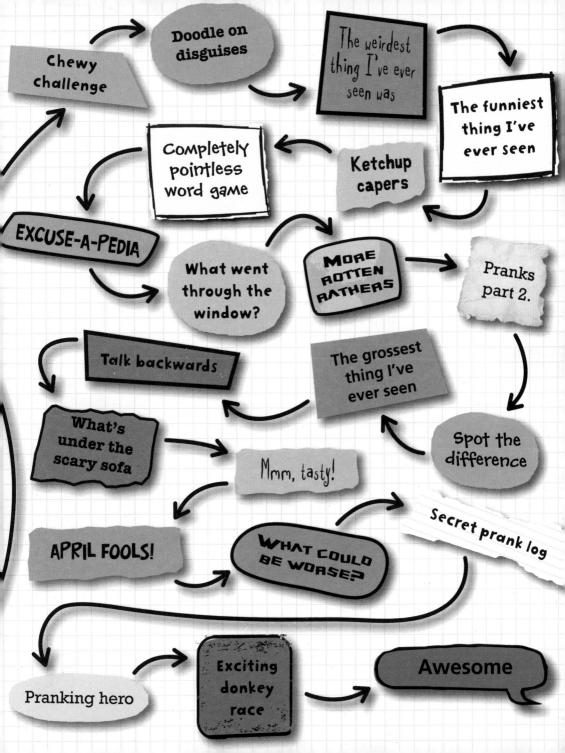

RULES OF PRANKING

1 Never play a prank on a complete stranger – you never know how they might react!

2 Pick your victims with care and consideration – pranking your 90-year-old neighbor is **not** funny but pranking your best friend *is* funny.

3 Most pranks require practice. Make sure you've perfected the prank before you spring the surprise!

4 If you play practical jokes, you have to be prepared to be pranked back. Make sure you can see the funny side!

5 Spread the fun! If you keep pranking the same person, your pranks will cease to be surprising!

6 If your prank is messy, clean up when it's over.

It's a **pranking** world!

Join two words to make a place name and doodle some in the signs.

Booger	wart
Wiffy	fluff
Putrid	spew
Dusty	ache
Zitty	scab
Nose	burp

4 ~~revolting~~ *delicious* pizza toppings

tomato and

and sausage

tuna and

and **ham**

Why did the **tomato** go to **Italy**?   It wanted **a pizza** the action!

NAME M

Write your name

then mash it up

by writing it backwards

or switching the letters around!

Your name:

_____

MASH IT!

_____

Now try mashing- up your friends' names!

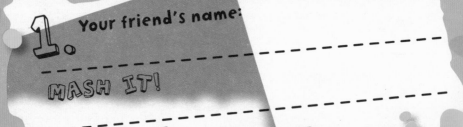

1. Your friend's name:

_____

MASH IT!

_____

2. Another friend's name:

_____

MASH IT!

_____

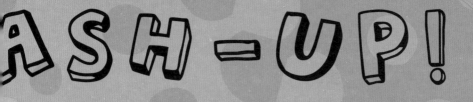

ASH-UP!

Gasp in wonder as plain old Jon Scott becomes **Noj Ttocs!**

3. And another friend's name:

MASH IT!

----

4. And another friend's name:

MASH IT!

----

5. So many friends. You rock!

MASH IT!

Hello there! Noj by name, Ttocs by nature.

Pranks Part 1.

1. YUMMY GUMMY

Gummy worms make great pranking tools. Make your folks a surprising snack by taking a nice big apple and making two or three holes in it. Let the apple stand for a couple of hours so the holes go nice and brown, then poke gummy worms into the holes and put the apple back in the fridge or fruit bowl. You'll **worm** your way into their hearts with this one!

Job done!

2. OH, BOO! THERE'S NO SHAMPOO!

Take a bottle of shampoo, remove the lid and place a piece of plastic wrap over the lip. Put the lid back on. When the next person goes to wash their locks, they'll wonder why the shampoo is stuck in the bottle!

shampoo

Job done!

3. PASTA PRANK

Next time your mom makes spaghetti, keep a few of the strings and let them get cold. When no one is looking, take your brother's or dad's shoes, remove the laces, and put them somewhere safe. Carefully replace the laces with the spaghetti. Alternatively, use strawberry or licorice laces for an even tastier trick!

Job done!

4. DUMB DRINK

Open a can of cola, drink it, and replace the liquid with cold soup. Offer your friend a drink, opening one for yourself at the same time so they think they hear the can opening. Watch in wonder as they slurp their **souper surprise!**

Cola

Job done!

POKE-in-the-eye DECISION-MAKER

Don't know who to prank?

Let the poke-in-the-eye pranking decision-maker decide for you!

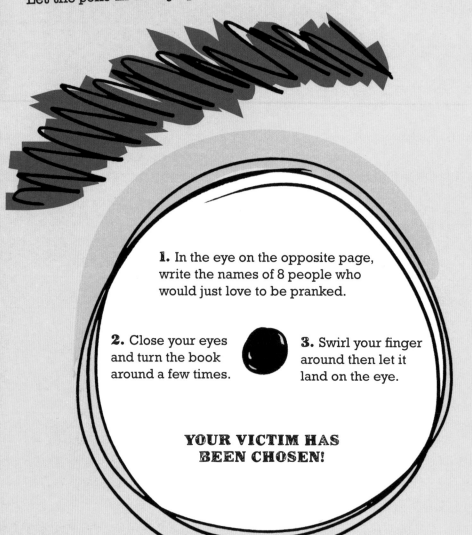

1. In the eye on the opposite page, write the names of 8 people who would just love to be pranked.

2. Close your eyes and turn the book around a few times.

3. Swirl your finger around then let it land on the eye.

YOUR VICTIM HAS BEEN CHOSEN!

Note: Never, ever poke a real person in the eye. Not fun, just dumb.

BLOW soccer

1. Cut out the straws on the opposite page. Roll them up and wrap tape around the top of each one to hold them together (and stop them from getting soggy).

2. Cut out the goalposts and place them about 7.8 in (20 cm) apart at either end of the table.

3. Cut out the ball and scrunch it up.

4. Place the ball in the middle of the table and use your straw to blow it into your opponent's goal.

5. If you want more rules, make them up yourself!

straws

Cut around the dotted lines.

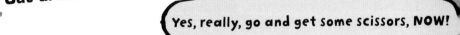

Yes, really, go and get some scissors, NOW!

goalposts

What's going on here?

Nothing. Go to the next page...

ball

YES! More cutting!

rotten rathers

Would you rather . . .

Have a cabbage-soup shower ☐
OR
a gravy bath? ☐

Have slugs in your gloves ☐
OR
put a fish down your pants? ☐

Mmmm! Delicious!

Sing in front of your school ☐
OR
dance in front of your football team? ☐

Wear a worm wig ☐
OR
knitted spaghetti underpants? ☐

BUGS on STRING

Plastic bugs are so much fun and guaranteed to bring joy wherever they go. Pump up the pranking potential by tying black thread to the bug. Place your bug where your victim can't miss it, hide, then pull the cord and watch the fun unfold.

Practice making the bug scamper quickly (quick pull), slither slowly (slow pull), or jolt forward (lots of quick, short pulls).

arrghhh!

arrghhh!

eeewww!

Under the door!

SPLAT that?

Cut out these nasty splats . . .

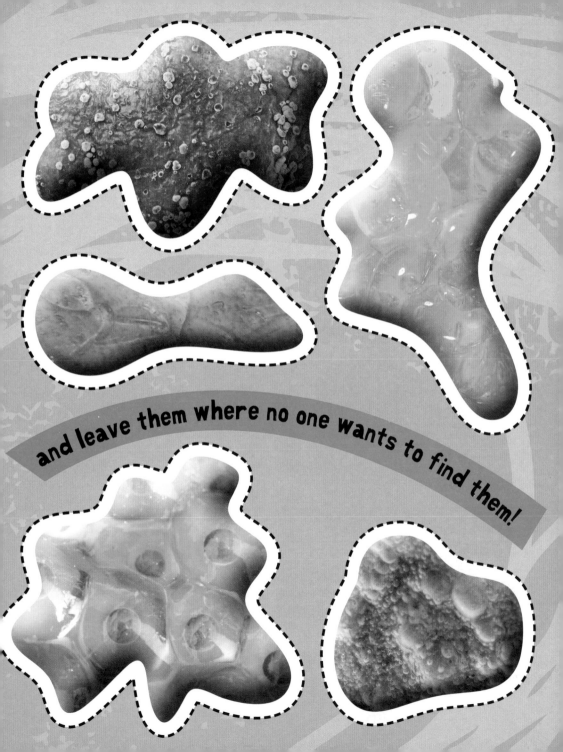

and leave them where no one wants to find them!

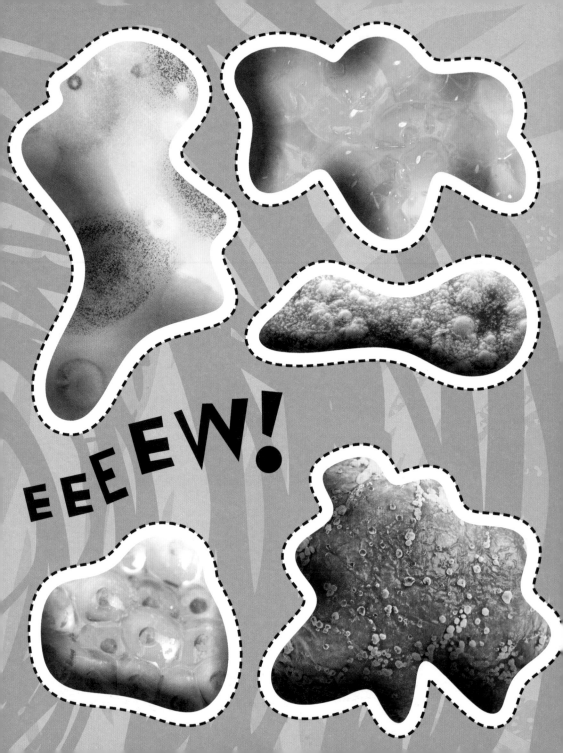

EEEEW!

Joke-a-pedia

Tape pages together with a Band Aid. Why? No idea.

laugh
your head...

72 quick-fire gags to treasure and share

1. Why did the boy keep his iPod in the fridge?

Because he liked cool music!

 /10

2. Which cats have eight legs?

Octopussies!

 /10

3. Why do pirates keep soap under their hats?

To help wash them ashore!

 /10

4. What's green and refuses to join in games?

The incredible sulk!

 /10

5. What do you call a bee in a bell tower?

A humdinger!

___/10

6. Did you hear about the scientist who broke the law of gravity?

He got a suspended sentence!

___/10

7. Why do storks stand on one leg?

Because they'd fall over if they lifted both!

___/10

8. What's a shark's favorite sandwich?

Peanut butter and jellyfish!

___/10

9. What's a hedgehog's favorite snack?

Prickled onions!

___/10

10. What's black and white and goes up and down?

A zebra in a lift!

___/10

11. How do you stop dogs chasing people on bikes?

Give them skateboards!

___/10

12. How do snowmen get to work?

On bICICLES!

___/10

13. Why do monsters eat metal pins?

It's their staple diet!

___ /10

14. Why couldn't the doctor see his patients?

Because he'd lost his glasses!

___ /10

15. What has a bottom at the top? *Your legs!*

___ /10

16. Where do pigs live?

In styscrapers!

___ /10

17. Why are skeletons afraid of the dark?

Because they've got no guts!

18. Which game is played with rotten eggs?

Ping-pong!

19. What do you call a man with gravy on his head?

Stew!

20. What kind of bugs do you find in libraries?

Bookworms!

21. What color is the wind?

Blew!

22. Why did the fireman's wife have a horrible Christmas?

Her husband put a ladder in her stocking!

23. Why do prank stars love chickens?

Because they are always telling yolks!

24. Why did the flea lose the singing contest?

Because he wasn't up to scratch!

25. Why did the apple run away?

Because the banana split!

26. Why do comic fans listen to the radio when they're driving?

They enjoy car toons!

27. Why did the rose go to university?
She was a budding genius!

28. What happened to the criminal who got locked in the freezer?

He became a hardened criminal!

29. Why are hairdressers never late for work?

Because they know all the shortcuts!

30. Why did the lady have her hair in a bun?

Because she'd eaten all her burgers!

31. What did the rock star do when he locked himself out?

He sang until he found the right key!

32. Why did the elephant miss his flight?

He spent too long packing his trunk!

33. Which animal should you never play with?

A cheetah!

34. Which vegetables will you find in a closet?

Jacket potatoes!

35. "Doctor, my nose is 11 inches long!"

"Come back if it grows into a foot!"

36. Why was the archaeologist depressed?

His career was in ruins!

37. How do toads guide their boats through the mist?

With frog horns!

38. What gets bigger the more you take away from it?

A hole in the ground!

39. Why were the company directors yawning?

They were having a bored meeting!

40. Why did the gray pebble buy bright purple trousers?

He wanted to be a little bolder!

41. What can you give and keep at the same time?

A cold!

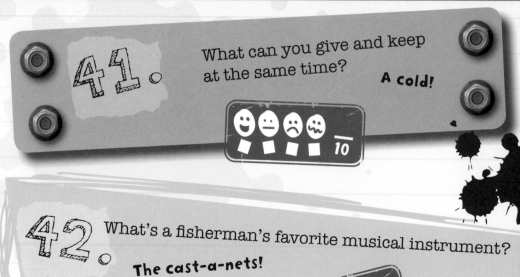

42. What's a fisherman's favorite musical instrument?

The cast-a-nets!

43. Why did the traffic light blush?

Because the trucks saw them changing!

44. What's the best snack to eat on a roller coaster?

F-RISE and dip!

45. What do you call a man with a car on his head?

Jack!

___/10

46. What jungle creature does Tarzan keep in his car?

Windshield vipers!

___/10

47. How did the gnome get indigestion?

By goblin his food!

___/10

48. How did the tap dancer break his leg?

He fell in the sink!

___/10

Hey, page 57, I'm gonna find you!

49. Where do barbers keep their money?

In shaving accounts!

$$2+5=7$$

$$6\div2=3$$

50. Why should you always wear glasses to do math?

Because they improve di-vision!

51. Did you hear about the sad man who lived next to a wall?

He never got over it!

52. Where do frogs keep their money?

In the river bank!

53. Where do crabs keep their money?

In the sand bank!

54. Did you hear about the man with size 18 boots?

Finding shoes was no small feet!

55. Did you hear about the man who didn't sit down for 27 days?

He couldn't stand it any longer!

56. Why doesn't gravity have many friends?

Because it brings everyone down!

Did you hear about the fire at the circus?

It was in tents!

Why is a calculator a faithful friend?

Because you can always count on it!

A PINK CALCULATOR!

YUCK!

Why did the store stop selling cardboard belts?

Because they were a waist of paper!

Did you hear about the mysterious well?

Nobody could get to the bottom of it!

61. Why did the boy take a photograph of his curtains?

Because drawing them was too difficult!

 /10

62. Why are mushrooms always invited to parties?

Because they are fun-guys!

 /10

63. Why are egg timers greedy?

Because they always go back four seconds!

/10

64. Why did paper dresses never catch on?

Because they looked just tear-able!

 /10

65. Why don't polar bears wear glasses?

Because they have good ice-sight!

66. What's green and sniffs?

A cucumber with a cold!

67. Did you hear about the calendar thief?

He got twelve months!

68. Why did the boy cover his hands in fertilizer?

He was trying to grow palm trees!

69.

How did the cyclist puncture his tire?

He drove over a fork in the road!

70.

What's red and hairy and goes up and down?

A raspberry in an elevator!

71.

What lives underground and uses bad language?

Crude oil!

72.

Why do fleas never pay train fares?

They prefer itch hiking!

itch itch

itch

itch itch

flea ville

Heard any good jokes?

Write them down here before you forget them!

More "ho-ho-ho" than a sleigh of Santas!

OK, the joke's over

Oops!

...off!

Doodle stuff coming out of the alien's nose

frightening FINGERS

Using a pencil, punch two holes though the Xs.

Wiggle your pencil until the holes are big enough to put your fingers through.

Turn the page over and **put your fingers through the holes**. Close the book.

Pick your victim and tell them you found something strange in your book, then **open it quickly** and reveal your dreadful digits!

chewy
challenge

Start here

Name: 　　　1

Name: 　　　2

Name: 　　　3

Name: 　　　4

1) Start chewing your gum. While you're chewing, pick a track and write your name next to the blob.

2) Once your gum is nice and soft, stick it on the blob and stretch it to the flag. Press it on the flag then stretch it back to the start. Then stretch it back to the flag. Then stretch it back to the start.

3) Keep going until your gum snaps. Record your lengths on the cup then challenge your friends.

Don't make your chewy **gooey!**

doodle on disguises

Give them names, if you must.

The weirdest thing I've ever seen was...

at home ○   at school ○   at my friend's house ○   somewhere else ○

It was...

green ○   red ○   brown ○   something else ○

It made me...

laugh ○   barf ○

Did you see that?

What was it?

....

Who else saw it?

....

Ketchup Capers!

Take your fake ketchup with you wherever you go.
It will be an endless **sauce** of fun!
Try putting it...

- on top of nice, clean washing. ☐
- on your mom's best chair. ☐
- on a freshly cleaned floor. ☐
- next to a plate of fries (see if anyone tries to dip in). ☐
- on a car seat. ☐
- on top of your dad's most expensive sweater. ☐
- next to a sandwich with a fake fly on top. ☐
- inside your dad's shoe. ☐
- on a fancy cushion. ☐
- in your sister's underwear drawer. ☐

Check the box when you've performed the prank!

Here are some ketchup jokes — they are really bad (and that doesn't mean good).

Why did the tomato sauce buy a Corvette?

He wanted to ketch up with the burger in a Porsche.

What did the sauce say to the sausage when it was too busy to talk?

I'll ketch up with you later!

(another)
COMPLETELY POINTLESS
WORD GAME

WRITE YOUR NAME or any other word.

Use the letters to make the dumbest word you can.

Think of more names and see how dumb you can be.

EXCUSE-A-PEDIA

Need an excuse? Try these! If you use an excuse too many times, people will not believe it, so keep track by checking the box every time you use it.

1   Oops! I didn't do my homework.

- Because I didn't want to make (*insert name*) look bad! ◯ ◯ ◯

- My little brother stole/ate it! ◯ ◯ ◯

- Aliens sneaked into my room and stole/ate it! ◯ ◯ ◯

- I had cheese stuck in my ear so I couldn't hear the teacher give the assignment! ◯ ◯ ◯

2   Oh, dear, my room is a mess!

- It's not a mess! It's ART! ◯ ◯ ◯

- I can't tidy up because disturbing the dust might upset my allergies! ◯ ◯ ◯

- It took me weeks to organize my things like this! ◯ ◯ ◯

- Aliens/my little brother sneaked in and messed it up! ◯ ◯ ◯

3 There is no way I am eating that!

Point at the window and shout, "What the heck is that?". While everyone turns to look, drop the offending food into a small bag for trashing later.

- I have a bad reaction to *(insert color)* food!

- This is so delicious, I must save some (nearly all of it) for *(insert name)*.

- Oh, no, my jaw's stuck! (For this you have to practice talking through your teeth.)

4 What a shame! I can't visit scary Aunt (insert name) because . . .

- I have an unexplained and incurable allergy to her lovely perfume!

- I have an essay to finish and I really must put my school work before pleasure. (Always impresses.)

- My dress clothes are in the wash and I can't go out without looking my best for Aunt *(insert name)*!

- I have not been well-behaved recently so I am grounding myself for a week. Oh, no! That means I can't visit Aunt *(insert name)*! Well, I'll just have to accept my punishment.

Or if you just need an excuse, one of these might do the job…

The doctor says I must take things easy if there is a Y in the day.

I'd love to, but I haven't a clue what you are talking about.

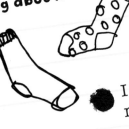

I have to stay in and match my socks.

I have to finish my cheese sculpture.

I have to measure my fingernails.

That would be way more fun than I deserve.

I did do it, but then the cosmos went backwards to a time when I hadn't done it.

I'm saving it as a treat for my 40th birthday.

Next door's cat ate it.

 I have to stay in and braid my nose hair.

I have to knit gloves for my goldfish.

I have to count the contents of a box of cornflakes.

**I'd love to, but the TV gets lonely
if I leave it alone for too long.**

Pet rock

 I have to stay in and
train my pet rock.

I need to catalog my navel-fluff collection.

I'm having friends over to watch water evaporate.

I have to lick the salt off my chips.

I have a rare reverse-hearing condition.
When you said, "Do," I thought you said, "Don't."

I'm staying in to practice counting back from a billion.

WHAT WENT THROUGH THE WINDOW?

CEREAL SURPRISE!

Offer to make your brother or sister breakfast.

Pour some cornflakes into a bowl then squirt some mayonnaise and ketchup on top.

Then pour some more cornflakes over the top (to hide the sauces) and add milk.

YUCK!

Watch their surprise as they munch on mayo!

YUCK!

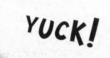

6. CEREAL SURPRISE 2!

Take the inner bag out of a cereal box and put it somewhere safe.

Fill half of the box with tiny balls of screwed up old newspaper.

See the joy on your victim's face as they pour their favorite morning meal!

CEREAL

7. SOCK SURPRISE!

If you made a few too many newspaper balls (or, hey, even if you didn't, why not make some more?), try sneaking some into your brother's socks.

Push some paper balls into the socks then neatly fold the socks back, and put them in his drawer.

Wait until he takes a pair from his drawer and lol as he wrestles with the rustling socks!

Job done!

8. JUST SAY THE WORD!

This prank works best if you team up with your brother or sister.

Before dinner, pick a word – it must be one that is likely to be used throughout the meal, like "please."

Every time your mom or dad says the word, cough really loudly or make a dumb noise.

This is guaranteed to annoy!

Job done!

cough!
PLEASE
Dee-da-da-dee!
cough!
PLEASE

SPOT THE DIFFERENCE

Two pictures of a horrible mess.
The same? Not quite.
Find **5** differences.

The grossest thing I've ever found:

1) Under my bed

In case you're interested, here's a picture of it. →

2) In my bed

3) In my ear

Yes, it was that bad. →

4) In my gym bag

Isn't that special? →

5) Under my fingernails

6) At the bottom of my drink

← This is 100% exactly what it looked like.

7) In my closet

8) On my shoe

← Still interested?

TALK BACKWARDS

Learning to talk backwards would probably take quite a long time, so learn these simple phrases to create a bit of early-morning pranking confusion.

Good morning, Mom and Dad. → daD dna moM gninrom doog

I seem to be talking backwards! → Sdrawkcab gniklat eb ot mees I

Can I have some toast? → Tsaot emos evah I nac?

Can I have some milk? → Kilm emos evah I nac?

Thank you → Uoy knaht

I don't understand. → Dnatsrednu t'nod I

Good-bye! → Eyb-doog!

SDRAWKCAB KLAT

Make your own backwards dictionary here.
Write what you want to say then write it backwards.

What's under the SCARY sofa?

Think of **5** things beginning with...

N
A
S
T
Y

Mmmm, tasty!

Doodle a topping on the pizza!

...ril Fools!

...asy pranks for that special day...

Achoo!

1. Put a little water in your hand and stand behind your victim. Cough, and flick the water at their neck. **Eeeew!**

Put a little honey on your brother/sister's door handle. **2.**

3. Wear your sweater backwards and act as though nothing's wrong.

4. Sneak in to the bathroom and wrap plastic wrap around the soap!

5. *Birth Certificate*

Tell your friends that your parents found your birth certificate and discovered you're three years older than you thought.

6. Separate your brother's socks and fold them back together in odd pairs.

Hee-hee! Hee-hee!

7. Put a piece of bread on a plate, sprinkle it with water so that it goes soft, then offer it to a friend. **YUCK!**

8. Tell your friends that you discovered you were born with green hair and your parents put special medicine in your cereal to keep it a "normal" color. See who believes you!

9. Reset your sister's ringtone to something really annoying.

10. Set an alarm clock to go off really early on Saturday morning and hide it in your brother's/sister's room.

What could be worse?

Start in the red box and follow the arrows filling in each box as you go.

Burnt toast — is better than → **sitting on a _____**

finding a _____ _____ in your school bag ← which would be better than

but not as bad as → **finding a _____ _____ in your shoe**

but not as scary as **having breakfast with a _____**

finding a _____ _____ in your bath which would be better than →

which is worse than

sitting in a bath of
_____

which is a picnic
compared to

going on holiday with a
_____

sharing a toothbrush with a
_____

which would be as gross as

having dinner with a
_____

or

which wouldn't be as bad as

finding a _____
_____ **in your bed!**

The end!

Secret Prank Log

Plan your pranking here and score your success out of 10!

Who? _____

When? _____

Prank _____ $\overline{10}$

Who? _____

When? _____

Prank _____ $\overline{10}$

Who? _____

When? _____

Prank _____ $\overline{10}$

Who? _____

When? _____

Prank _____

ha-ha!
ha-ha!

10

Who? _____

When? _____

Prank _____

10

Who? _____

When? _____

Prank _____

10

Who? _____

When? _____

Prank _____

10

Who? _____

When? _____

Prank _____

arghh!

10

Who? _____

When? _____

Prank _____

10

Who? _____

When? _____

Prank _____ 10

Who? _____

When? _____

Prank _____ 10

Who? _____

When? _____

Prank _____ 10

hee-hee!

ha-ha!

Who? _____

When? _____

Prank _____

_____

ha-ha!

gotcha!

$\overline{10}$

_____

Who? _____

When? _____

Prank _____

$\overline{10}$

Who? _____

When? _____

Prank _____

_____

$\overline{10}$

Who? _____

When? _____

Prank _____

$\overline{10}$

Who? _____

When? _____

Prank _____

$\overline{10}$

arghh!

arghh!

Who? _____

When? _____

Prank _____

$\overline{10}$

Stick a picture of your head here
then draw yourself as the
pranking hero,
you know you are.

Right, so there is no page 57!

Gotcha!

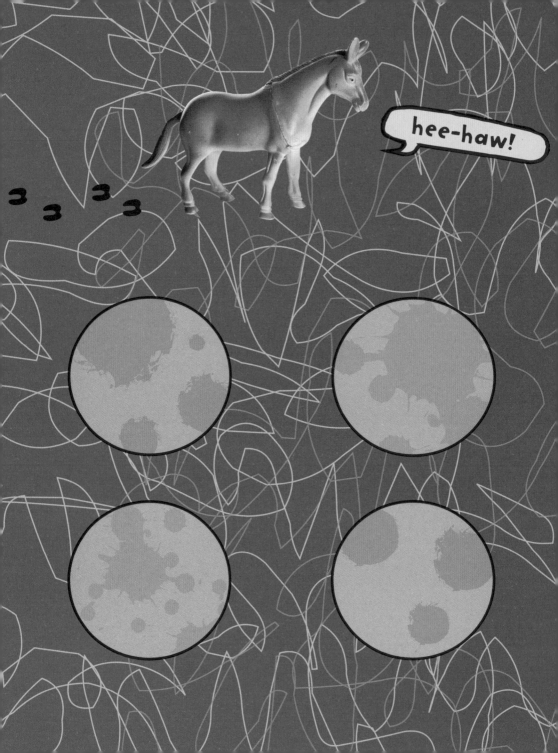

Just when you thought it couldn't get more exciting!

Back
3

Forward
4

Miss two turns!

Forward
5

Forward
6

1) Pick a donkey, cut it out, and place it on the start position.

2) Roll a dice and work your way around the track. How thrilling is that?

3) When you land on an instruction, you must do as it says (until you think of a better use of your time).

4) Keep going around the track until you land on the finish line.

Go back to the start.

Back
3

Forward
4

Back
2

Ha-ha miss a turn!